Kid's Box

BOX

New Generation

British English

Caroline Nixon &
Michael Tomlinson

CAMBRIDGE

Activity Book
with Digital Pack

4

Thanks and acknowledgements

Authors' thanks

Many thanks to everyone at Cambridge University Press for their dedication and hard work, and in particular to: Liane Grainger and Lynn Townsend for supervising the whole project and guiding us calmly through the storms.

Eve Conway for her astute observations and great editorial judgement. Thanks for all the hard work and great result.

We would also like to thank all our pupils and colleagues, past, present and future, at Star English academy in Murcia, especially Jim Kelly for his friendship and support throughout the years.

Dedications

For Teresa and Giuseppe Vincenti, for their wholehearted support and encouragement, with much love and thanks. – CN

To my great friends from the Levante: to Javi, Maria José and Laura, and to Jim Kelly. It's always a pleasure to spend time with good friends. – MT

The authors and publishers acknowledge the following sources of copyright material and are grateful for the permissions granted. While every effort has been made, it has not always been possible to identify the sources of all the material used, or to trace all copyright holders. If any omissions are brought to our notice, we will be happy to include the appropriate acknowledgements on reprinting and in the next update to the digital edition, as applicable.

Key: U = Unit

Photography

The following photos are sourced from Getty Images.

U0: U0: ajaykampani/iStock/Getty Images Plus; Chris Stein/Stone; kali9/iStock/Getty Images Plus; MileA/iStock/Getty Images Plus; roevin/Moment; Василий Авраменко/iStock/Getty Images Plus; Malcolm MacGregor/Moment Open; Paulo Amorim/Moment; Peter Cade/Stone; Tomwang112/iStock/Getty Images Plus; PhotoAlto/Thierry Foulon/PhotoAlto Agency RF Collections; PeopleImages/iStock/Getty Images Plus; Ariel Skelley/DigitalVision; Boy_Anupong/Moment; Oscar Wong/Moment; **U1:** Jim Zuckerman/The Image Bank; Kiyoshi Hijiki/Moment; lechatnoir/E+; BLOOM image; Blend Images - REB Images/Tetra images; Paul Starosta/Stone; Kim Sayer/The Image Bank Unreleased; JGI/Tom Grill/Tetra images; Ariel Skelley/DigitalVision; Rick Gomez/Tetra Images; SDI Productions/E+; moodboard/iStock/Getty Images Plus; mikroman6/Moment; Anna Erastova/iStock/Getty Images Plus; **U2:** Nadezhda1906/iStock/Getty Images Plus; Ratchapoom Anupongpan/EyeEm; AGF/Contributor/Universal Images Group; Alan Thornton/The Image Bank; Alistair Berg/DigitalVision; Jupiterimages/BananaStock/Getty Images Plus; SeventyFour/iStock/Getty Images Plus; Mike Svoboda/DigitalVision; Mayur Kakade/Moment; Jose Luis Pelaez Inc/DigitalVision; kali9/E+; Westend61; Andersen Ross Photography Inc/DigitalVision; Soren Hald/Image Source; Stockbyte; Thomas Barwick/Stone; David Arky/Tetra images; Nick David/DigitalVision; Peter Dazeley/The Image Bank; Paul Starosta/Stone; Peerayot/iStock/Getty Images Plus; miflippo/iStock/Getty Images Plus; Isabella Antonelli/EyeEm; Anna Erastova/iStock/Getty Images Plus; nazlisart/iStock/Getty Images Plus; **U3:** PonyWang/E+; Anna Erastova/iStock/Getty Images Plus; **U4:** SolStock/E+; kickstand/iStock/Getty Images Plus; studo58/iStock/Getty Images Plus; Rubberball/Nicole Hill/Brand X Pictures; Nafiz Rahat/iStock/Getty Images Plus; Jon Lovette/Stone; Vadzim Kushniarou/iStock/Getty Images Plus; martin-dm/E+; Dmytro Aksonov/E+; Stockbyte; Mehmet Hilmi Barcin/iStock/Getty Images Plus; andresr/E+; uchar/iStock/Getty Images Plus; Itziar Aio/Moment; Kseniya Sharapova/Moment; Anna Erastova/iStock/Getty Images Plus; alla_snesar/iStock/Getty Images Plus; Yukobo/iStock/Getty Images Plus; Olena Poliakevych/iStock/Getty Images Plus; **U5:** Youst/DigitalVision Vectors; romrodinka/iStock/Getty Images Plus; Anna Erastova/iStock/Getty Images Plus; **U6:** FG Trade/E+; Radomir Jovanovic/E+; Joseph Rodriguez/EyeEm; Anna Erastova/iStock/Getty Images Plus; **U7:** SCIEPRO/Science Photo Library; John T. L. Williams Photography/Moment; Arturo de Frias photography/Moment; beccarie/iStock/Getty Images Plus; skynesher/E+; Robbie Ross/iStock/Getty Images Plus; kavram/iStock/Getty Images Plus; Peter Adams/Stone; Martin Harvey/The Image Bank; Amy Brinkerhoff/EyeEm; Nnehring/E+; bbevren/iStock/Getty Images Plus; Anna Erastova/iStock/Getty Images Plus; nazlisart/iStock/Getty Images Plus; **U8:** GeorgeDolgikh/iStock/Getty Images Plus; Brian Hagiwara/The Image Bank; Sommai Larkjit/EyeEm; Rodica Ciorba/500px; ShutterWorx/E+; george tsartsianidis/iStock/Getty Images Plus; Ghislain & Marie David de Lossy/Image Source; Photo By Gervanio Guimaraes/Moment; Wavebreak/E+; Mehmet Hilmi Barcin/iStock/Getty Images Plus; Nettiya Nithascharukul/EyeEm; ER Productions Limited/DigitalVision; FatCamera/E+; Dan Brownsword/Image Source; gemphotography/iStock/Getty Images Plus; Ann Spratt/EyeEm; Eva-Katalin/E+; shunli zhao/Moment; daizuoxin/iStock/Getty Images Plus; Picnote/iStockphoto/Getty Images; Anna Erastova/iStock/Getty Images Plus; nazlisart/iStock/Getty Images Plus.

The following photos are sourced from other libraries.

U1: Eugenio Marongiu/Alamy Stock Photo;

Commissioned photography by Copy cat and Trevor Clifford Photography.

Illustrations

Adam Linley (Beehive); Antonio Cuesta; Carol Herring (The Bright Agency); Ilias Arahovitis (Beehive); Marek Jagucki; Michael McCabe (Beehive); Leo Trinidad (The Bright Agency)

Cover Illustration by Pronk Media Inc.

Audio

Audio production by Creative listening.

Design and typeset

Blooberry Design

Additional authors

Katy Kelly: Lock's Sounds and Spelling.

Rebecca Legros: CLIL.

Freelance editor

Emma Ramirez

Contents

Hello there! 4

1 Back to school 10

Art: How can we use paint? 16

2 Good sports 18

Sport: What urban sports can we do? 24
Review: units 1 and 2 26

3 Health matters 28

Career-related learning: What makes
a job fun? 34

4 After school club 36

Maths: What can a survey tell us? 42
Review: units 3 and 4 44

5 Exploring our world 46

Geography: How can I stay safe outdoors? 52

6 Technology 54

Technology: How does technology help us? 60
Review: units 5 and 6 62

7 At the zoo 64

Science: How are life cycles different? 70

8 Let's party! 72

Literature: How can we write poetry? 78
Review: units 7 and 8 80

Values 82

Units 1 & 2 Value others 82
Units 3 & 4 Be kind 83
Units 5 & 6 Be safe 84
Units 7 & 8 Recycle 85
Grammar reference 86
Irregular verbs 88

Hello there!

1 Read and circle.

1 Their dog's (dirtier) / **cleaner** than their cat.
2 Grandpa Star's **younger** / **older** than Mr Star.
3 Stella's **taller** / **shorter** than Suzy.
4 Aunt May's hair is **shorter** / **longer** than Uncle Fred's hair.
5 Mr Star's **smaller** / **bigger** than Simon.
6 Grandma Star's **happier** / **sadder** than Mrs Star.

2 Read and complete.

1 Lily wants to play _____badminton_____ .
2 Jim wants to go _____ .
3 Vicky and Peter want to _____ .
4 Sally wants to _____ .
5 Daisy wants _____ .
6 Fred and Paul _____ .
7 Charlie _____ .

Language: revision

📱 Do the online activities on Practice Extra as you complete this unit.

Sort and write the words. Complete the crossword.

1

olcd

2

augnhty

```
c  l  e  v  e  r
h
i
l
d
r
e
n
```

3

nhguyr

4

dlou

5

sthrtiy

6

~~lcveer~~
clever

7

uqiet

8

itrde

2 **Read and complete the Kid's Box File.**

My name's _____ .

I'm _____ years old. I've got _____ hair

and _____ eyes.

There are _____ people in my family.

They are called _____

_____ .

I like _____ and _____ .

I don't like _____ .

My favourite _____ is _____ .

Ask your friend. Complete the questionnaire.

1	Do you wake up at six o'clock?	always	☐	sometimes	☐	never	☐
2	Do you have breakfast in the kitchen?	always	☐	sometimes	☐	never	☐
3	Do you have lunch at school?	always	☐	sometimes	☐	never	☐
4	Do you watch TV after school?	always	☐	sometimes	☐	never	☐
5	Do you go to bed at nine o'clock?	always	☐	sometimes	☐	never	☐
6	Do you go to the park at the weekend?	always	☐	sometimes	☐	never	☐

 Write about your friend.

1 My friend Peter always wakes up at six o'clock.
2 My friend _____ has breakfast _____ .
3 My _____ has _____ .
4 My _____ watches _____ .
5 _____ goes _____ .
6 _____ .

 Read and match.

Hello, Jack. How are you?

1

c

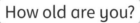

How old are you?

2

☐

What's your name?

3

☐

Who's that?

4

☐

Whose glasses are those?

5

☐

Whose tractor is that?

6

☐

a They're my aunt's.   c I'm fine, thanks.   e I'm ten.
b That's my uncle, Paul.   d It's my uncle's.   f I'm Mary.

Look and complete with 'before' or 'after'. Match.

  **a**

  **b**

 **f**

 **c**

1 She gets up _after_ she wakes up. ☐ b

2 She washes _____ she has breakfast. ☐

3 She gets dressed _____ she washes. ☐

4 She has breakfast _____ she cleans her teeth. ☐

5 She combs her hair _____ she gets her bag. ☐

6 She catches the bus _____ she puts on her shoes. ☐

 **e**

 **d**

Circle the odd one out.

1 (trousers)   cleaner   doctor   dentist   farmer
2 floor   door   window   stairs   bus
3 library   hospital   supermarket   cinema   lorry
4 bear   snake   rock   lion   bat
5 river   lake   sea   blanket   waterfall
6 plant   grass   cook   tree   leaf
7 son   aunt   driver   uncle   daughter
8 sunny   hot   island   windy   cloudy
9 builder   scarf   hat   sweater   coat
10 longer   quieter   teacher   shorter   bigger

Lock's sounds and spelling

1 **Say and underline the sounds using the correct colour.**

c<u>u</u>rly   pl<u>ay</u>   r<u>i</u>des

c<u>u</u>rly   pl<u>ay</u>   r<u>i</u>des   night   thirsty   day

kites   five   sometimes   nurse   always   bike   girls

2 **Read and complete with words from Activity 1. Write one more sentence.**

1 In the afternoon, the farmer is a**lways** th**irsty** .

2 In the morning, the c_____-haired n_____ eats eggs.

3 The doctor s_____ r_____ a b_____ to work.

4 During the d_____, the detectives p_____ together until n_____ .

5 F_____ g_____ fly k_____ in the evening.

6 _____

3 **Circle the odd one out. Use the other words to make sentences.**

1 ride / white / (curly) / sometimes / bike
    I sometimes ride a white bike.

2 stay / play / night / always / day
    _____

3 five / dirty / bird / thirsty / nurse
    _____

   Sounds and spelling: *-ur, -ir, -ay, -i* and *-igh* spellings

1 Read and write the numbers. Then join the dots in the correct order and answer.

Start with picture 68. Find another picture with the same object. Look, there's a flower in 68 and there's a flower in 39. Now find the next picture and write the number.

68	39										

What is the picture? _____

Remember to complete the online activities for this unit on Practice Extra .

Vocabulary: numbers

9

Back to school

1 **Find and circle the words.**

busy   exciting   boring   careful   difficult   ~~brave~~   slow   quick   terrible

d	z	e	x	s	b	r	a	v	e	a
i	p	h	c	u	f	b	m	e	v	r
f	w	w	a	r	j	i	m	x	c	e
f	z	a	r	p	j	n	f	c	r	k
i	n	l	e	r	e	s	p	i	n	p
c	q	h	f	i	k	l	q	t	p	e
u	u	b	u	s	y	o	h	i	g	u
l	i	j	l	e	i	w	l	n	f	h
t	c	g	b	o	r	i	n	g	d	k
u	k	r	t	e	r	r	i	b	l	e

2 **Look at the pictures in Activity 1. Complete the sentences.**

1   The woman's fighting the fire. She's very **b**rave_____.

2   My mum is **b**_____ because she works a lot.

3   My aunt thinks television is **b**_____.

4   This book is very **e**_____. I don't want to go to bed.

5   My younger sister thinks it's **d**_____ to put her shoes on.

6   What a great motorbike. It's really **q**_____!

7   You must be **c**_____ when you cross the road.

8   We were at the beach yesterday. It was windy and cold.
    The weather was **t**_____.

9   The snail is a small animal. It's very **s**_____.

▶ Do the online activities on **Practice Extra** as you complete this unit.

Complete the questionnaire.

Me

1	I think Music lessons are	boring. ☐	easy. ☐	exciting. ☐
2	I think television is	exciting. ☐	terrible. ☐	boring. ☐
3	I think Maths lessons are	easy. ☐	difficult. ☐	exciting. ☐
4	I think football is	exciting. ☐	boring. ☐	terrible. ☐
5	I think computer games are	terrible. ☐	exciting. ☐	difficult. ☐
6	When I do my homework, I am	careful. ☐	quick. ☐	slow. ☐
7	When I go to school, I am	quick. ☐	slow. ☐	careful. ☐

2 **Ask your friend. Write the answers.**

What do you think of computer games?

I think they're exciting.

1 What do you think of computer games? _exciting_
2 What do you think of television?
3 What do you think of tennis?
4 What do you think of school?
5 What do you think of pop music?
6 What do you think of comics?
7 What do you think of football?

1 🎧 2 **Listen and draw lines. Colour.**

Paul | Jane | Mr Edison | Peter | Mary | Jim

2 **Read and circle.**

1 This is the person **when** / (**who**) / **when** teaches children.
2 There **are** / **is** / **have** five children in the classroom.
3 Mr Edison is the teacher **what** / **when** / **who** is writing on the board.
4 Mary is the girl **where** / **with** / **who** is wearing a pink dress.
5 Paul's book is **in** / **under** / **on** the desk.
6 Jim is the boy **who** / **with** / **why** is sharpening his pencil.
7 Peter is talking **about** / **to** / **for** Mary.
8 In the classroom, the children **must** / **can't** / **mustn't** listen to the teacher.

Language: relative clauses with *who*

Look at the pictures. Read and correct.

black beard

1 The man who's painting has got a ~~grey moustache~~.
2 The man who's throwing a ball has got a little white dog.
3 The woman who teaches Music lives in a big house.
4 The man who's wearing a green sweater rides his horse to school.
5 The woman who likes books gets up at nine o'clock.

Read and complete the table. Label the pictures.

There are four new teachers at KB Primary School.

Name	Description	Age	Subject	Hobby
		42	English	
Miss Stone				
		28		playing the guitar
	curly grey hair		Music	

1 The woman who teaches Music likes reading. She's 57.
2 The teacher who's called Mr Brown has got a black beard. He is 42.
3 The woman who's 30 has got long fair hair. She teaches Maths.
4 The man who likes playing the guitar has got a brown moustache.
5 The man who likes playing tennis teaches English.
6 The woman who teaches Maths likes horse riding.
7 The man who doesn't teach English teaches Sport. His name's Mr Kelly.
8 The woman who's 57 is called Mrs Bird.

1 Sort and write the words. There's one extra letter in each word.

1 ncetigiex   *exciting*   6 sasey
2 cikiqu   7 vbeare
3 ribonrg   8 subsy
4 owsls   9 lefaclru
5 icdfiltduf   10 etirbirle

2 Complete the table with the words from Activity 1. Colour the stressed syllable.

	Syllable 1	Syllable 2	Syllable 3
1	ex	cit	ing
2			
3			
4			
5			
6			
7			
8			
9			
10			

3 Write adjectives to complete the sentences for you. Circle the stressed syllable in each adjective.

1 I think riding a bike is _____.
2 Playing outside is always _____.
3 Learning at school is sometimes _____.
4 When I do sport, I'm _____.
5 The weekends are always _____.
6 My best friend is _____.

Movers Reading and Writing

1 🐵 **Read the story. Choose a word from the box. Write the correct word next to numbers 1–5. There is one example.**

My name is Sally. My dad's a _____farmer_____ and I live on a big farm in the country. We've got about eighty **(1)** _____ and thirty cows. My dad's always busy and he sometimes works at **(2)** _____ ! On Saturdays and Sundays, I sometimes help my dad with the animals.

I don't want to be a farmer. I want to be an Art **(3)** _____ . I study Art at school, but I only have two lessons a week and I want to **(4)** _____ better pictures.

Every Friday afternoon, after school, my aunt and I catch the bus to the city centre. My aunt goes shopping and I have another longer Art class. It's never **(5)** _____ , it's exciting!

boring	sheep	school	night	tiger

teacher	farmer	draw	pretty

(6) **Now choose the best name for the story. Tick one box.**

Sally wants to be a farmer ☐

Sally goes shopping with her aunt ☐

Sally wants to be an Art teacher ☐

How can we use paint?

  Read and circle the adjectives.

1 The painting uses (bright) happy colours.
2 The artist uses curved lines to make interesting shapes.
3 The colourful round shapes make the painting look attractive.
4 The painting reminds me of pink lemonade.
5 I feel excited when I see the painting.

Plan

 Go back to Pupil's Book page 17.

2 Read again and complete. Make notes about another painting.

Artist	Piet Mondrian	
Title of painting	Composition in blue, red and yellow	
Style		
Adjectives to describe the painting		
Adjectives to describe your feelings about the painting		

Write **Write a description of the painting. Use your notes.**

Edit **Did you ...**

☐ write about the artist's style in your description?
☐ use descriptive adjectives to describe the painting?
☐ say how the painting makes you feel?

Writing Tip
Include descriptions that help the reader imagine what you are talking about.

Do you remember?

1 **Read and write the words.**

1 She's Stella's friend, but she's older than her.   Meera

2 A person who works in a hospital.

3 The opposite of 'always'.

4 A person who looks at teeth every day.

5 There are a lot of these in a forest. Monkeys sometimes live in them.

6 The opposite of 'difficult'.

7 This little animal is very slow.

 2 **Cross out the words from Activity 1.**

new	~~Meera~~	dentist	likes	doctor	teacher
never	Lenny	snail	trees	his	easy

Use the other words to write a sentence.

 3 **Read and write 'T' (true) or 'F' (false).**

1 Lock and Key go to Peter's school on Tuesday.   F

2 Lock tells the class that detectives find people and things.

3 Lock and Key eat lunch at the school.

4 The teacher thinks Lock and Key's work is boring.

5 Lock and Key play football after lunch.

6 The teacher thinks Lock and Key are naughty.

 # Can do

I can describe people.

I can describe things.

I can say what I think.

2 Good sports

1 🎧 3 **Listen and draw lines.**

Jane

Jim

Mary

Fred

Jack

Daisy

Peter

2 **Write the sentences in order.**

(tennis) (I) (difficult.) (think) (is)

1 _____ I _____ think _____ tennis _____ is _____ difficult._____

(learn) (skateboard.) (to) (can) (We)

2 _____

(She's) (who) (ice skating.) (the girl) (likes)

3 _____

(play) (can) (You) (inside.) (basketball)

4 _____

(you) (fishing?) (want) (Do) (to go)

5 _____

📱 Do the online activities on Practice Extra as you complete this unit.

Read and complete the table.

Paul, Metin, Amira and Beth are at the sports centre. They want to learn how to do different things.

Name	Age	Sport	Equipment
			a big ball
		swim	
Amira			
	12		

1   The boy who's twelve wants to learn to climb. He needs strong shoes and a helmet.
2   Beth wants to learn to swim so she needs a towel.
3   Beth and Paul are both twelve.
4   Metin is eleven and Amira is ten.
5   The girl who's ten wants to learn to roller skate. She needs some roller skates and a helmet.
6   The boy who's eleven wants to play volleyball. He needs a big ball.

Read and write the words.

1   What do we call people who teach?   teachers
2   What do we call people who dance?
3   What do we call people who climb?
4   What do we call people who swim?
5   What do we call people who ice skate?
6   What do we call people who win?
7   What do we call people who sing?

1 Read and circle. Match.

1 She's writing **careful** / **(carefully)**. [a]
2 They're running **quickly** / **quick**. [ ]
3 I'm drawing **bad** / **badly**. [ ]

4 You're walking **slow** / **slowly**. [ ]
5 He's reading **well** / **good**. [ ]
6 We're speaking **quietly** / **quiet**. [ ]

2 Read and complete for you.

> badly   well   slowly   quickly   carefully   loudly   quietly

1 I sing _badly_ .
2 I play tennis ___ .
3 I write ___ .
4 I read ___ .
5 I ride my bike ___ .

6 I eat ___ .
7 I drink ___ .
8 I sometimes walk ___ .
9 I play the guitar ___ .
10 I sometimes talk ___ .

3 Now ask a friend.

> Do you sing badly?

> No, I sing really well.

4 Read. Sort and write the words.

1 A place where you can practise football inside. (ecstrponerts)   sports centre
2 A place where you can fish. (ervri)
3 A place where you can skateboard. (akprtseka)
4 A place where you can ice skate. (ikcreni)
5 A place where you can climb trees. (efrsto)
6 A place where you can swim in the sea. (abceh)

Read and match.

1 We're shouting loudly

a because your school bus is going.

2 She's talking quietly

b because she doesn't want to drop them.

3 He's walking slowly

c because I'm drawing very badly.

4 You're running quickly

d because he's got a backache.

5 They're winning

e because she's in the library.

6 She's carrying the boxes carefully

f because they're playing well.

7 I need an eraser

g because we're watching an exciting football game.

 Read and complete the table.

	swim	play football	play the piano	sing	write	climb	draw
Alex							
Meera							
Lenny		well	badly				
Suzy							
Simon							
Stella							

1 The person who plays football well plays the piano badly.
2 The person who swims quickly sings quietly.
3 The person who writes well swims slowly.
4 The person who sings loudly writes slowly.
5 The person who plays the piano well climbs carefully.
6 The person who climbs quickly draws well.

Lock's sounds and spelling

1 Find and circle the words.

(skip)skatesportswimswingslothskirtspiderskateboard

2 Read and complete. Use words from Activity 1.

1
 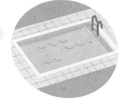

The _sloth_ wants to learn to _____ .

2

The _____ wants to learn to _____ .

3

The _____ wants to learn to _____ .

4

The _____ wants to learn to _____ .

3 Look and write sentences.

1   The sloth swings.

2 _____

3 _____

4 _____

Movers Listening

1 🎧 4 🐵 **Listen and colour and write. There is one example.**

What urban sports can we do?

 Read and underline the adverbs.

1 The players <u>carefully</u> move a small disc with a long, special stick.
2 If you're not careful, you can hurt yourself badly.
3 You need to throw the ball quickly at the wall.
4 It's a difficult game to play well.

Plan Go back to Pupil's Book page 25.

 Read again and complete. Make notes to invent a new urban sport.

Name of game	Bottle Bounce	
Number of players	2–4	
How to get ready to play		
How to play and win		

Write   **Make a poster about your new urban sport. Use your notes.**

Edit   **Did you …**

☐ include the name of the game?
☐ say how many people can play?
☐ explain how to get ready to play?
☐ say how to play and win the game?
☐ include pictures?

Writing Tip

Use pictures to go with your text. It helps if people can see what you are describing.

Do you remember?

1 Complete the crossword.

What's this sport? _____

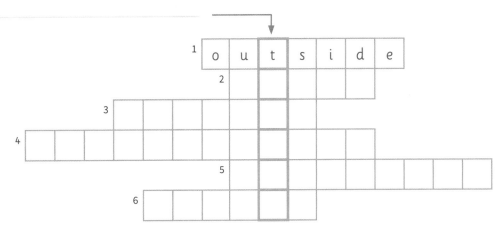

1 | o | u | t | s | i | d | e |

1 The opposite of 'inside'.
2 Hair on a man's face. It's under his mouth.
3 Grandpa Star loves going to the river to catch fish. He loves ... .
4 We can play games, run and jump here.
5 The opposite of 'easy'.
6 A person who paints pictures.

2 Read and match.

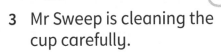

1 The swimming coach is asking Key to come quickly. ☐ c
2 The swimming coach is shouting loudly. ☐

3 Mr Sweep is cleaning the cup carefully. ☐
4 Mr Sweep is shouting at Key angrily. ☐

 a
 b
 c
 d

Can do

I can say more action verbs.

I can talk about how I do things.

I can talk about learning new things.

1 **Read and answer.**

1 What's the second letter in ?   a

2 What's the second letter in ?

3 What's the fourth letter in ?

What's the word?

4 What's the first letter in   ?

5 What's the third letter in ?

6 What's the first letter in ?

7 What's the second letter in ?

8 What's the fourth letter in  ?

2 **What's wrong with these pictures? Write sentences.**

1  The bat's got a long beard.

2

3

4

5

6

Circle the odd one out.

1 (eight)	first	second	third
2 skip	quick	jump	roller skate
3 well	badly	slowly	tall
4 busy	careful	holiday	terrible
5 earache	Music	Sport	Maths
6 class	teacher	weather	school
7 thirty	first	ninety	forty
8 running	jumping	shopping	swimming
9 family	aunt	uncle	beard
10 skip	famous	difficult	exciting
11 hair	moustache	beard	climb
12 bike	run	swim	hop

 Use the words from Activity 3 to complete the crossword. Write the message.

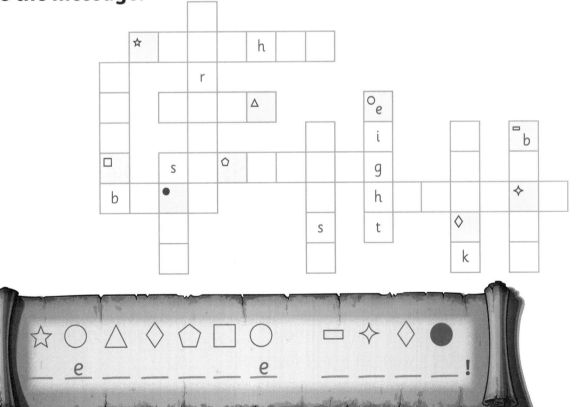

☆ ○ △ ◇ ⬠ □ ○   ▭ ✦ ◇ ●

_ e _ _ _ _ _ e _   _ _ _ _ !

3 Health matters

1 **Read Stella's diary.**

> Friday
>
> I had a busy day. In the morning, I ate a big breakfast and drank a lot of milk. I went to school with Suzy. Before lunch, I had my favourite lessons, Maths and Science. I saw my Music teacher and took her my project. It's my new song. After lunch, our English teacher gave us an exam. There were 20 questions. I was the first to finish!

Now look for the past tense of these verbs.

1 is   was
2 have
3 eat
4 drink
5 go

6 see
7 take
8 give
9 are

2 **Read and complete. Use the past tense verbs from Activity 1.**

> After school, I ¹ went   to the library. There
> ² _____ lots of new books about famous people.
> I ³ _____ my Science teacher at the library.
> She ⁴ _____ me a book on Marie Curie and I
> ⁵ _____ another book on detectives for Simon.
> He ⁶ _____ at home in bed because he
> ⁷ _____ a cold. We ⁸ _____ fish
> and chips for dinner and I ⁹ _____ some more milk
> before I went to bed. I love milk!

📱 Do the online activities on Practice Extra as you complete this unit.

1 Read, choose and circle. Compare with your friends.

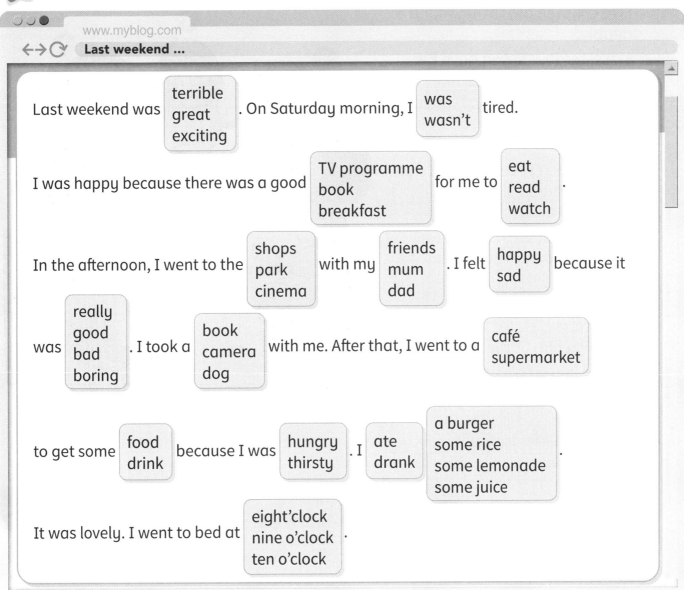

www.myblog.com

← → C **Last weekend ...**

Last weekend was [terrible / great / exciting] . On Saturday morning, I [was / wasn't] tired.

I was happy because there was a good [TV programme / book / breakfast] for me to [eat / read / watch] .

In the afternoon, I went to the [shops / park / cinema] with my [friends / mum / dad] . I felt [happy / sad] because it was [really good / bad / boring] . I took a [book / camera / dog] with me. After that, I went to a [café / supermarket]

to get some [food / drink] because I was [hungry / thirsty] . I [ate / drank] [a burger / some rice / some lemonade / some juice] .

It was lovely. I went to bed at [eight'clock / nine o'clock / ten o'clock] .

 2 Now write about last weekend.

Last weekend was

Read and complete the table.

Five children are sitting round a table.

- Yesterday, Susan gave her mum some flowers. She didn't have lunch at school. She's sitting between Paul and Jack.
- Paul didn't see his friends yesterday. He did his homework.
- Daisy went to a party. She didn't go to the cinema.
- The girl who didn't go to a party or give her mum flowers is called Sally. She saw a film at the cinema.
- The boy who's sitting next to Sally had a stomach-ache, so he didn't eat any food.
- Sally didn't drink any milk at breakfast.

	Name	(+) Yesterday, he / she …	(-) Yesterday, he / she …
1		went to a party	didn't go to the cinema
2			
3	Jack		
4	Susan		
5			didn't see his friends

Write sentences about the children.

1 Daisy went to a party. She didn't go the cinema.

2

3

4

5

Language: past simple irregular verbs: affirmative and negative

1 Put the words in groups.

chicken cousin burger teacher mum
milk school lemonade hospital banana
cinema juice park water nurse apple

Places: _____

People: _____

Food: chicken _____

Drink: _____

2 Decide what Meera did yesterday. Choose and write words from Activity 1.

	go	see	eat	drink
morning	hospital			
afternoon		cousin		
evening				

3 Ask and answer. Complete the table with your friend's answers.

Did Meera go to the hospital in the morning? Yes, she did.

Did she see the nurse? No, she didn't.

	go	see	eat	drink
morning				
afternoon				
evening				

1 Read and complete with 'b' or 'v'. Then look and circle 'True' or 'False'.

1 There's a b ig b ird with a ___ag of ___egetables.   True / **False**

2 At the ___each, two ___oys are playing ___ase ___all.   True / False

3 The ___rown ___ear and the ___et are eating ___urgers.   True / False

4 A spider is sleeping in a ___ery ___ig ___ed.   True / False

2 Draw things with the letters 'b' and 'v'. Write sentences.

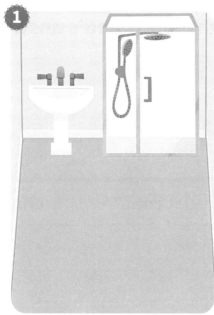

There's a _____ in the bathroom.

Movers Listening

1 🎧 5 😊 **Listen and write. There is one example.**

At the doctor's

	When?	yesterday
1	What was the matter?	ache
2	Can't eat:	
3	Where was her aunt on Friday?	
4	Her temperature:	
5	She has to:	

What makes a job fun?

Practise

1 **Read and circle the pronouns. Then write the contractions.**

1 I am a video game designer.   I'm

2 They are a lot of fun to create. _____

3 We are all friends in my band. _____

4 It is fun when we play together. _____

Plan

Go back to Pupil's Book page 35.

2 **Read again and complete. Make notes for your dream job.**

	Joaquín's dream job	Your dream job
Job title	musician	
Description		
Training		
What makes the job fun?		

Write

3 **Write a blog entry about your dream job. Use your notes.**

Edit

4 **Did you ...**

☐ give your blog a title?

☐ describe the job?

☐ use contractions?

☐ say what training you need for the job?

☐ say what makes the job fun?

☐ add your personal blog name?

Writing Tip

Use contractions in your blog to make your writing style informal.

Do you remember?

1 **Match to make sentences.**

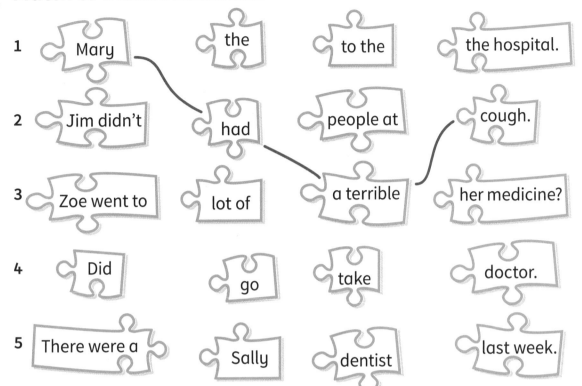

1 Mary · the · to the · the hospital.

2 Jim didn't · had · people at · cough.

3 Zoe went to · lot of · a terrible · her medicine?

4 Did · go · take · doctor.

5 There were a · Sally · dentist · last week.

2 **Read and tick.**

1	Did Key visit his aunt in hospital?	Yes, he did. ✓	No, he didn't.
2	Did Key see Nick Motors in the hospital café?	Yes, he did.	No, he didn't.
3	Did Lock and Key go to the hospital by car?	Yes, they did.	No, they didn't.
4	Did Key think the doctor was Nick Motors?	Yes, he did.	No, he didn't.
5	Did Nick Motors take the motorbike?	Yes, he did.	No, he didn't.
6	Did Lock and Key catch Nick Motors?	Yes, they did.	No, they didn't.

Can do

I can talk about health matters.

I can talk about the past.

I can ask questions about the past.

4 After school club

 1 Read and complete. Use the past tense of the verbs.

Kim and Sally had a great weekend. They went to an activity centre in the countryside with their friend Paul.

On Saturday morning, they ¹ ___started___ (start) early. First, they ² _____ (sail) on the lake. Then, in the afternoon, they ³ _____ (climb) a mountain. In the evening, they ⁴ _____ (cook) burgers outside. The children ⁵ _____ (talk) and ⁶ _____ (laugh) all evening.

On Sunday morning, they ⁷ _____ (walk) in the forest. Their teacher ⁸ _____ (plant) a tree and Kim, Sally and Paul ⁹ _____ (help) him.

In the afternoon, they ¹⁰ _____ (play) games. They ¹¹ _____ (want) to stop at four o'clock because they ¹² _____ (need) to go home and sleep!

2 Read and write 'yes' or 'no'.

1 Kim and Sally had a boring weekend.   no
2 On Saturday morning, they sailed on the lake
3 In the evening, they cooked burgers inside.
4 On Sunday afternoon, they walked in the forest.
5 Their teacher planted a tree.
6 In the afternoon, they played the trumpet.
7 They stopped at five o'clock.
8 They needed to go home and sleep.

Complete the table with the past tense of the verbs.

~~like~~ ~~try~~ ~~stop~~ ~~sail~~ play jump drop invite skate
close shop cry skip shout dance climb carry hop

+ed	+d	+ped	~~y~~+ied
sailed	liked	stopped	tried

Write the secret message.

¹ was	² at	³ supermarket	⁴ he	⁵ I	⁶ shouted
⁷ He	⁸ motorbike	⁹ and	¹⁰ laughed	¹¹ Motors	¹² outside
¹³ him	¹⁴ tried	¹⁵ but	¹⁶ jumped	¹⁷ the	¹⁸ Nick
¹⁹ and	²⁰ our	²¹ to	²² pointed	²³ on	²⁴ catch

I tried

LOCK,

5-14-21-24-18-11.
7-1-12-17-3. 5-22-2-13-
9-6, 15-4-10-19-16-23
20-8!

KEY

1 Match and write.

fifth	5th
_____	3rd
_____	2nd
_____	9th
_____	1st
_____	12th
_____	20th
_____	8th

first   second   third   eighth   fifth   ninth   twentieth   twelfth

2 Read and write three words starting with each letter.

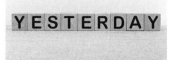

1 The ninth letter of 'toothpaste'.
   tired, temperature, Thursday

2 The eighth letter of 'baseball'.

3 The fourth letter of 'naughty'.

4 The tenth letter of 'downstairs'.

5 The sixth letter of 'outside'.

6 The second letter of 'yesterday'.

7 The fifth letter of 'strong'.

8 The third letter of 'kick'.

Look and complete. Who was the winner?

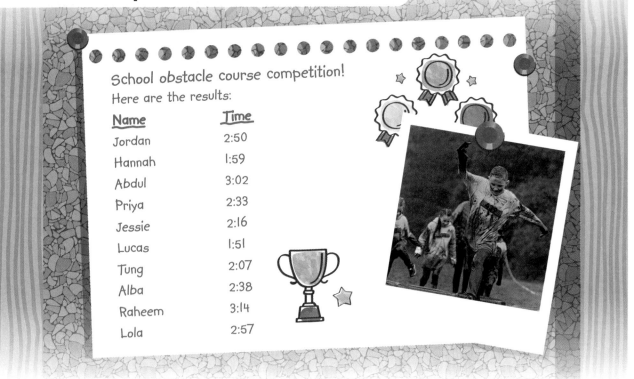

School obstacle course competition!
Here are the results:

Name	Time
Jordan	2:50
Hannah	1:59
Abdul	3:02
Priya	2:33
Jessie	2:16
Lucas	1:51
Tung	2:07
Alba	2:38
Raheem	3:14
Lola	2:57

_____ was first.   _Priya_ was fifth.   _____ was ninth.
_____ was second.   _____ was sixth.   _Raheem_ was tenth.
Tung was third.   _____ was seventh.
_____ was fourth.   _Lola_ was eighth.

Read and complete the table.

Jim, Daisy, Vicky and Fred were in different competitions last weekend.
One danced, one ice skated, one jumped and one played table tennis.
Vicky was fourth in her competition and Jim was third in his.
Daisy jumped in her competition.
Fred danced in his competition.
The boy who came third played table tennis.
The girl who didn't ice skate came first.

Name	Position	Activity
Daisy		
	second	
Vicky		ice skated

Lock's sounds and spelling

1 **Say and write the past tense verbs in the correct box.**

> ~~start~~ ~~help~~ ~~carry~~ want dance laugh
> jump rain play invite like clean

△	T	□
started	helped	carried

2 **Read and complete with past tense verbs from Activity 1.**

Last Sunday, it ¹□ _rained_ so I was at home. First, I ²□ _____ my room and then I ³T _____ my sister tidy her room. My sister ⁴△ _____ to bake a cake, but I ⁵△ _____ my best friend to my house. We ⁶T _____ to our favourite song and ⁷T _____ loudly. We had so much fun! We ⁸□ _____ kangaroos and ⁹T _____ around the living room. Then, my dad ¹⁰△ _____ making dinner and we ¹¹□ _____ the plates to the table for everyone. I really ¹²T _____ my rainy day at home last Sunday!

3 **Write about last Sunday. Draw △, T or □ above the *-ed* endings.**

Movers Listening

1 🎧 6 🐵 **Listen and tick (✓) the box. There is one example.**

What did Daisy do on Saturday?

A ☐   B ✓   C ☐

1 Who did Daisy go to the park with?

A ☐   B ☐   C ☐

2 What time did they go to the park?

A ☐   B ☐   C ☐

3 What did Daisy and her friends do first?

A ☐   B ☐   C ☐

4 What did they have for lunch?

A ☐   B ☐   C ☐

5 How did Daisy and her friends go home?

A ☐   B ☐   C ☐

What can a survey tell us?

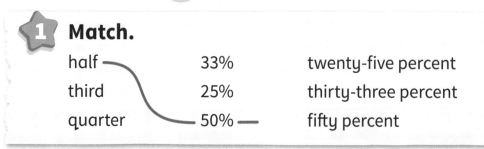

1 Match.

half	33%	twenty-five percent
third	25%	thirty-three percent
quarter	50%	fifty percent

Plan

Go back to Pupil's Book page 43.

2 Read again. Number in order of popularity.

1 = most popular; 5 = least popular

☐ football   1 games   ☐ tennis

☐ drama   ☐ running

Write

3 **Do your own survey and make notes. Write a report.**

Survey title	
Introduction	
Most popular	
Least popular	
Other interesting information	

Edit

4 Did you ...

☐ include a title?

☐ write an introduction?

☐ say what the most and least popular things are?

☐ include percentages?

> **Writing Tip**
>
> At the beginning of a sentence, write numbers in words instead of figures. *Ten* percent say Maths is their favourite subject.

Do you remember?

1 **Read and circle. Complete the email.**

1	phone	(phoned)	phones	5	climb	climbed	climed
2	us	we	our	6	fifteenth	fifteen	fiveteenth
3	afternoon	two o'clock	Saturday	7	called	cleaned	cooked
4	talk	play	listen	8	waved	watched	washed

From: simon@kidsbox.com   **To:** fred@kidsbox.com

On Wednesday, Alex ¹ _phoned_ me. He invited ² _____ to go to his house on ³ _____ to ⁴ _____ about the school show.
We walked to Alex's house with Meera and Lenny. We ⁵ _____ up to the ⁶ _____ floor. His mum ⁷ _____ fish for lunch. Then we ⁸ _____ a film on television. It was very funny.

2 **Read and correct the sentences.**

1 Peter has ~~four~~ *two* tickets for his school show.

2 Pupils and teachers are in the show.

3 Lock and Key are sitting in the seventh row.

4 Key buys two milkshakes.

5 Nick Motors is a pirate in the show.

6 Lock pulls Peter's dad's hair.

Can do

I can say the numbers 1st to 20th.			
I can talk about things I did yesterday.			
I can ask questions about last week.			

Review Units 3 and 4

1 Find and circle the past tense of the verbs.

~~are~~ have go take see
eat drink give wash
try is like fish skate

s	k	a	t	e	d	w	s	f	l	m
w	w	t	s	g	d	a	y	i	i	h
e	t	w	b	a	d	s	h	s	k	a
n	s	o	r	v	w	a	s	h	e	d
t	h	c	o	e	t	r	i	e	d	n
d	r	a	n	k	g	e	o	d	o	a
e	o	w	e	r	e	p	t	a	t	e

2 Read and complete with past tense verbs from Activity 1.

1 Jim _____went_____ to the hospital to see his grandmother.

2 Sue _____ a lot of water because she was thirsty.

3 Peter _____ sick last week so he _____ the doctor.

4 Vicky _____ a bad cold so she _____ some medicine last night.

5 Mary and Sally _____ ill yesterday because they _____ a lot of chocolate.

6 Fred _____ his mother some flowers for her birthday.

3 Read and write 'Yes, I did' or 'No, I didn't'.

1 Did you go to the cinema last Saturday? _____

2 Did you get up early yesterday? _____

3 Did you play basketball last week? _____

4 Did you need a scarf yesterday? _____

5 Did you dance last weekend? _____

Circle the odd one out.

1 headache   (moustache)   earache   backache
2 had   phoned   went   gave
3 between   behind   awake   down
4 quickly   worse   slowly   carefully
5 neck   back   shoulders   kick
6 ate   drank   closed   saw
7 hurt   first   second   eighth
8 cry   carry   sailed   try
9 skip   danced   jump   hop
10 shouted   needed   writes   started
11 thirty   forty   sixty   twentieth
12 tired   pointed   started   shouted

 Use the words from Activity 4 to complete the crossword. Write the message.

Exploring our world

 1 Read and match.

1 The explorer found
2 He caught a lot
3 They came
4 She took some
5 We made a
6 They got up at
7 I lost my
8 You could
9 They had
10 They went

a photos of polar bears.
b five o'clock in the morning.
c camp in the forest.
d a map, but they got lost.
e home two months after the start of the expedition.
f of fish in the lake.
g sailing in a small boat.
h map so I didn't know where to go.
i a new island.
j drink water from snow when you were thirsty.

2 Make a wordsearch.

Write seven verbs here:

find
can

Write the past tense of each verb in the wordsearch. Complete the wordsearch with other letters.

c										
o			f	o	u	n	d			
u										
l										
d										

 3 Now find the past tense verbs in your friend's wordsearch.

Language: past simple irregular verbs

[▶] Do the online activities on Practice Extra as you complete this unit.

1 Look. Ask and answer.

Could Vicky swim when she was three?

No, she couldn't.

Could Vicky swim when she was five?

Yes, she could.

2 Tick or cross the boxes for you. Then ask and answer with three friends.

Could you walk when you were one?

No, I couldn't.

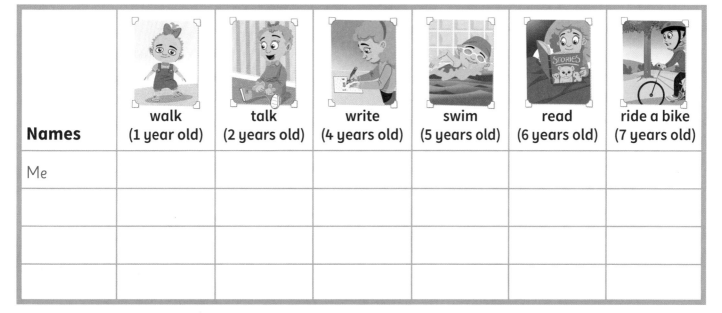

Names	walk (1 year old)	talk (2 years old)	write (4 years old)	swim (5 years old)	read (6 years old)	ride a bike (7 years old)
Me						

3 Read and match.

1 He couldn't find his toothpaste
2 She couldn't find her glasses
3 He couldn't find his coat
4 I couldn't find my gloves
5 We couldn't find our books
6 She couldn't find her phone

so

a we didn't do our homework.
b I had cold hands.
c she couldn't talk to her friend.
d he couldn't clean his teeth.
e she couldn't read her book.
f he had to wear a jacket.

Language: *could* and clauses with *so*   47

1 Complete the crossword.

What's the opposite of … ?

1 interesting
2 difficult
3 good
4 straight (hair)
5 clean
6 wrong
7 last
8 quietly
9 new

| b | o | r | i | n | g |

What's the secret word?

 2 Read and match.

1 Peter's test is more difficult than Vicky's.
2 This film is more exciting than that one.
3 The programme about snails is more boring than the one about sharks.
4 She's more famous than him.
5 She carried the plates more carefully than him.
6 Her homework is better than his.

Look and write sentences.

thirsty   careful   happy   famous   ~~hungry~~   strong   dirty

1   Simon's hungrier than Stella.
2   _____
3   _____
4   _____
5   _____
6   _____
7   _____

 Compare Tom's days. Choose words from the box.

the weather (good / bad / sunny)   Tom (hungry / happy / tired)
the lesson (exciting / boring / difficult)

Wednesday   Sunday

Tom was hungrier on
Wednesday than on Sunday.

1 **Complete the words with 'ir' / 'ur' / 'or'.**

w o r d   f _ st   c _ _ cus

sk _ t   w _ k   th _ sty   b _ _ ger

w _ ld   t _ n   th _ d   g _ l

2 **Read and complete with words from Activity 1.**

1 The t h i r s t y girl drank three cups of water.

2 My brother always eats a _____ at the restaurant.

3 I want to fly around the _____ in a big balloon.

4 The clown at the _____ was very funny.

5 My mum goes to _____ every morning at eight o'clock.

6 Betsy didn't win the race, she came _____.

7 Turn around and show me your new _____.

3 **Circle the four words you didn't use in Activity 2. Use them to write sentences.**

1 _____

2 _____

3 _____

4 _____

Movers Reading and Writing

1 🐵 **Read the text. Choose the right words and write them on the lines.**

Blue Whales

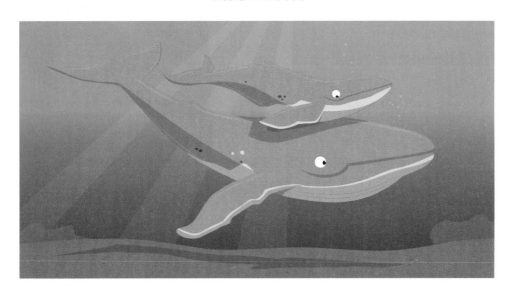

Example	Blue whales are blue or grey and _____they_____ live in all the
1	oceans in the world. They _____ very small sea animals,
	small fish and plants. Blue whales are bigger than all other animals.
2	_____ bodies are longer than two buses and they've
3	_____ very big mouths. About a hundred people can
4	stand in a blue whale's mouth! On _____ first day of its
5	life, a baby blue whale is bigger _____ a grown-up hippo.
	It drinks about four hundred litres of milk every day and it grows
	very quickly.

Example	it	she	they
1	eat	eating	ate
2	Her	His	Their
3	got	get	getting
4	the	a	some
5	then	that	than

How can I stay safe outdoors?

Practise

 Read and circle the imperatives.

1 (Use) a warm sleeping bag at night.
2 Don't eat big meals.
3 Eat plenty of vegetables.
4 Wear warm clothes.
5 Don't go outside with wet hair.

Plan

Go back to Pupil's Book page 53.

 Read again and complete. Write safety tips for cold weather.

Safety tips for hiking in hot weather	Safety tips for hiking in cold weather
Drink lots of water.	
Wear sun cream.	

Write

 Write a leaflet with safety tips for hiking in cold weather. Use your notes.

Edit

 Did you ...

☐ give your leaflet a title?
☐ include a list of 'dos and don'ts'?
☐ add pictures?

Writing Tip

Use lists to present key information in a clear way.

Do you remember?

1 **Read and match. Colour the squares.**

It's mine.

It's their garden.
yellow

They're yours.

It's ours.

They're his trees.
pink

They're his.

They're hers.

It's my bike.
green

It's our world.
red

It's theirs.

They're your maps.
purple

They're her plants.
blue

2 **Read and number Nick Motors' actions in order.**

a He ate breakfast at the Lakeside restaurant.

b He escaped on Lock and Key's bike.

c He caught a bus to the holiday camp. [1]

d He sent a message to Lock's phone.

e He had dinner at the Lakeside restaurant.

Can do

I can talk about events in the past.

I can compare people and things.

I can say sentences with 'so'.

6 Technology

1 Read and complete.

> screen   apps   internet   ~~email~~   laptop

From: isabella@dmail.com   To: emily@efl.com

Subject: Cool birthday present!

Hi Emily!

How are you? I'm writing you this ¹ _email_ on my new ² _____.
I got it yesterday for my birthday! Mum and Dad said I can use the
³ _____ to find out information for school and to email my friends.
I also downloaded some cool ⁴ _____ – one for playing music and
another one for watching video clips. The ⁵ _____ is quite big so it's
like watching TV! Oh, and I can also read e-books on it. Do you know any
good ones?

Are you free this afternoon? Do you want to go roller skating
in the park?

Love, Isabella ♥ 😃

2 Read and circle.

KBX4 instructions

1 To turn on the laptop, you push the **mouse** / **screen** / (**button**).

2 To find your place on the screen, you move the **internet** / **DVD** / **mouse**.

3 You can write **an app** / **an email** / **a TV** to your friend using the **button** / **keyboard** / **DVD**.

4 You can look for information on the **mouse** / **internet** / **button**.

5 You can also download **screens** / **apps** / **DVDs** from the internet.

📱 Do the online activities on **Practice Extra** as you complete this unit.

 **Listen and write. There is one example.**

Shopping

1 John went shopping with his mum and *dad* _____ .

2 They bought _____ .

3 It's for _____ .

4 He needs it to _____

_____ .

5 It cost £ _____ .

 Write the sentences in order.

1 (years ago.) (There weren't) (a hundred) (any mobile phones)

There weren't any mobile phones a hundred years ago.

2 (use it.) (before you can) (You have to turn) (the laptop on)

_____

3 (to text your friends) (It's easier) (emails.) (than to send)

_____

4 (You can use) (to text) (your friends.) (a mobile phone)

_____

5 (listen to) (on our computers.) (We can) (music)

_____

6 (than paper books.) (and smaller) (E-books) (are better)

_____

7 (use the internet) (We can) (on our mobile phones.)

_____

Vocabulary: technology 55

Match and write the past tense verbs. Use each verb to write a sentence.

1 bo *ught*

2 ga

3 w

4 ca

5 th

6 c

7 d

8 p

9 kn

10 ch

id

aught

ught

ought

ew

ent

ve

ose

ut

me

1 I bought a T-shirt from the shop.

2

3

4

5

6

7

8

9

10

 Tick six words. Play *Bingo*.

buy	☐	get	☐	have	☐	see	☐
catch	☐	bring	☐	is	☐	say	☐
choose	☐	go	☐	put	☐	take	☐
come	☐	know	☐	read	☐	think	☐

BINGO!!! BINGO!!! BINGO!!! NGO!!! BINGO!!! NGO!!! BINGO

1 **Read and write the numbers.**

1 Defne had forty-seven computer games. She gave her younger brother fifteen and her older brother gave her twelve. How many has she got now?

forty-four

2 Farmer Green had eleven lemon trees and twenty orange trees. He bought eight more lemon trees on the internet. How many trees did he have then?

_____

3 Grandpa bought a new fishing video. Then he went fishing. He caught thirty-two fish, but he dropped eight in the river. How many fish did he take home?

_____

4 Jordan had twenty-five apps on his mobile phone. He bought nineteen more apps on the internet. He deleted four apps because he didn't like them. How many apps has he got now?

_____

 2 **Read and match the questions and answers.**

1 What did they give their mother for her birthday?

2 Why did he put on his coat?

3 When did she take these photos?

4 Which floor did they go up to?

5 Who did you see yesterday afternoon?

6 How many fish did Grandpa catch?

7 What time did you get up last Friday?

a They went up to the twelfth floor.

b We got up at eight o'clock.

c They gave her a red scarf.

d Because it was cold outside.

e He caught four.

f I saw my aunt.

g She took them last weekend.

Lock's sounds and spelling

1 Complete the words with 'ou' / 'or' / 'a'. Write the words in the correct box.

f or k   sm a ll   th ou ght   f __ r   sp __ t
br __ ght   t __ ll   t __ lk   b __ ght   w __ ter
c __ lled   sh __ t   w __ lked

OO

thought

O

fork

△

small

2 Read and correct the sentences.

1   We ~~worked~~ to the new computer shop.   *walked*

2   Did you toulk to your grandpa yesterday?

3   My favourite spart is tennis.

4   I thorght she liked computer games.

5   Mum braght pizza home for dinner.

6   My sister is very tall, but I am shout.

3 Use the words that aren't in Activity 2 to write sentences. Draw OO, O or △ above the words.

1 _____

2 _____

3 _____

4 _____

Movers Listening

1 🎧 8 **Where did Charlie go with these people?**
Listen and write a letter in each box. There is one example.

 Mum

 Aunt Daisy ☐

 Dad ☐

 Lily ☐

 Grandma ☐

 Fred ☐

A

B

C

D

E

F

G

H

How does technology help us?

 Practise **1** Underline the regular past tense verbs and circle the irregular past tense verbs.

1 A Scottish man <u>invented</u> the first TV.
2 The first mobile phones were big and heavy.
3 He heard the word 'robot' in a play.
4 People listened to music on 'personal stereos' in the past.
5 Everybody read on paper.

Plan

Go back to Pupil's Book page 61.

 2 Read again and complete. Make notes for another inventor.

Inventor	George Devol	
Best invention		
What did it do?		
Other inventions		

 Write **3** 📝 Write a biography of an inventor. Use your notes.

 Edit **4** Did you ...

☐ include details about the inventor?
☐ include details about his or her invention(s)?
☐ use regular and irregular verbs in the past?

Writing Tip
Include dates in your biography to support facts.

Do you remember?

1 Match to make sentences.

1 We go — loves

2 I couldn't use a — to the

3 She — email their

4 He bought — a new

5 They wanted to — laptop

6 You read — some

cousin in — was three.

computer for — on holiday.

when I — his mum.

texting — India.

e-books — every Saturday.

cinema — her friends.

 ## 2 Read and circle.

1 A man (came) / wrote onto Miss Rich's boat and read / took her money.
2 The bag of money saw / was on the table.
3 Lock and Key went / bought to Miss Rich's boat in a rowing boat.
4 Nick Motors heard / wrote an email and Lock read / thought it.
5 Key listened / saw Nick Motors taking their rowing boat.

Can do

I can write 'technology' words.

I can talk about computers and the internet.

I can say more verbs in the past.

Review Units 5 and 6

1 **What can you see? Tick the boxes.**

moon ☐   orange ☐   river ☐   snail ☐   cage ☐   plant ☐

sweater ☐   blanket ☐   glass ☐   comic ☐   road ☐

cup ☑

beard ☐   bottle ☐

dog ☐   laptop ☐

picnic ☐   sun ☐

leaves ☐   rock ☐

email ☐

parrot ☐   banana ☐

moustache ☐

toothbrush ☐   rabbit ☐   grown-up ☐   uncle ☐

2 **What can't you see? Write the words.**

1   uncle   4 _____   7 _____
2 _____   5 _____   8 _____
3 _____   6 _____

3 **Find the word. Use the first letters from Activity 2.**

c ☐ ☐ ☐ u ☐ ☐ ☐

Circle the odd one out.

1	bought	thought	brought	(sailed)
2	ticket	button	mouse	screen
3	plant	DVD	keyboard	app
4	better	dirtier	quickly	funnier
5	bounced	between	behind	above
6	sharks	bears	whales	dolphins
7	river	cave	sea	ocean
8	drank	swam	liked	gave
9	Wednesday	evening	Sunday	Friday
10	was	were	went	where
11	weather	hotter	colder	quicker
12	came	made	found	know

 Use the words from Activity 4 to complete the crossword. Write the message.

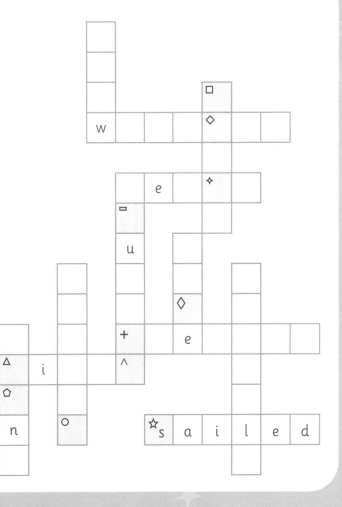

7 At the zoo

1 **Make sentences.**

~~The polar bear~~	lives	in	world.
Penguins	the loudest	sea	the forest.
The dolphin can't	drink	animal in the	~~on land.~~
The blue whale is	live	~~meat-eating animal~~	Antarctica.
The parrot	~~is the biggest~~	in	water.

1   The polar bear is the biggest meat-eating animal on land.

2 _____

3 _____

4 _____

5 _____

2 **Read and complete.**

father   mother   sister   brother   grandfather   aunt

In the giraffe family, [1] _____ aunt _____ giraffe is the most beautiful.
[2] _____ giraffe is the tallest. [3] _____ giraffe is the youngest
and [4] _____ giraffe is the oldest . The cleverest giraffe in the family is
[5] _____ giraffe. [6] _____ giraffe is the loudest giraffe in
the family.

Language: superlative adjectives   Do the online activities on **Practice Extra** as you complete this unit.

Read and write the animals.

1 This is the tallest animal. It's got four legs and a very long neck.
   giraffe

2 It's the biggest land animal. It's got two very big ears. _____

3 Some people think this is one of the most beautiful animals. It can fly. _____

4 This is the best animal at climbing trees. It can be very naughty too. _____

5 This is the most dangerous animal. It can also swim. _____

6 This is the quickest animal here. It can also climb trees. _____

 Ask your friends. Write the answers.

Ask four friends about their family.

60%

	1	2	3	4
1 Who's the oldest in your family?				
2 Who's the youngest?				
3 Who's the quietest?				
4 Who's the strongest?				
5 Who's the tallest?				
6 Who's the best at drawing?				
7 Who's the worst at singing?				
8 Who's the loudest?				

Language: superlative adjectives   65

1 9 **Listen and write the letter.**

2 **Make a wordsearch.**

Write seven verbs here:

drive

fly

_____

_____

_____

Write the past tense of each verb in the wordsearch. Complete the wordsearch with other letters.

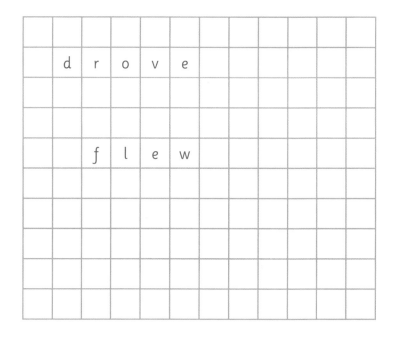

3 **Now find the past tense verbs in your friend's wordsearch. Write three sentences with the past tense verbs.**

1 _____

2 _____

3 _____

Language: past simple irregular verbs

What did the animals do? Read and complete.

> flew   slept   ran   sat   ~~ate~~   swam

1 The lizard _____ate_____ the fly.
2 The tiger _____ into the tall grass to play.
3 The parrot _____ round the bird house.
4 The dolphin _____ quickly round the big round pool.
5 The monkey _____ in the tall tree.
6 The polar bear _____ next to the big square pool.

 Read and complete with 'into', 'out of', 'along' or 'round'.

1 The train came _____out of_____ the station.
2 They flew _____ the bear's head.
3 Peter went _____ the library.
4 Mary came _____ the hospital.
5 The sharks swam _____ the island.
6 The cat walked _____ the wall.

1 Complete the words with 'ew' / 'ue' / 'oo'. Circle the sounds using the correct colour.

f(oo)t   dr(ew)   sch__l   g__d   bl__   z__

fl__   t__k   l__k   p__l   resc__   w__d

2 Look and describe the picture to your friend.

> There are some monkeys at school.

> Yes, and there's a hippo in a blue pool.

3 Read and complete.

> foot   good   baboon   ~~rescue zoo~~   blue birds
> wood   school   blue pool

Today, we're at the ¹ ___rescue zoo___ . There are monkeys at ² _____ learning Art with a ³ _____ . There are ⁴ _____ flying over a big tree. Look! There's a bear hiding in the ⁵ _____ – I can see his ⁶ _____ . The hippo is in the ⁷ _____ . He's very ⁸ _____ at swimming! What a great day at the rescue zoo!

Movers Reading and Writing

1 🐵 **Read the text and choose the best answer.**
Sally is talking to her friend Jack.

Example

Sally: What are you reading, Jack?

Jack: A No, I'm not.
⒝ A book about animals.
C I'm writing.

Questions

1 Sally: Do you like animals?

Jack: A I haven't got a dog.
B No, thanks.
C I love them.

2 Sally: Which is your favourite animal?

Jack: A Whales are the ugliest.
B I really love tigers.
C I don't like chocolate.

3 Sally: Why do you like them?

Jack: A I think they're the most beautiful animals.
B I don't think so.
C I'd like some chips, please.

4 Sally: Did you go to the zoo last week?

Jack: A Yes, we went on Friday afternoon.
B Yes, we do.
C Yes, every Saturday.

5 Sally: What did you do there?

Jack: A We see the elephants.
B We don't see the lions.
C We saw the kangaroos.

6 Sally: Hmm. Do you want an apple?

Jack: A Yes, please. I like apples.
B OK. What colour?
C Yes, a banana.

How are life cycles different?

Practise **1** Read and complete with a full stop (.) or an exclamation mark (!).

1 The bowhead whale lives in the Arctic Ocean ⬚.
2 It can live to be 200 years old ⬚
3 It's a mammal ⬚
4 They can be 20 metres long and weigh over 100,000 kilograms ⬚
5 Whales are the heaviest animals on Earth ⬚

Plan ⬅ Go back to Pupil's Book page 71.

2 Read again and complete. Make notes for another animal.

Name	Greenland shark	
Animal group	fish	
Where it lives		
Lifespan		
What it eats		
Amazing facts		

Write **3** 📝 Write a report about your animal. Use your notes.

Edit **4** Did you ...

⬚ include some amazing facts in your report?
⬚ use exclamation marks after your amazing facts?

Writing Tip
Include amazing facts when you write a science report. Your report will be more fun to read!

Do you remember?

1 ## Read and match the questions and answers.

1 Did the kitten sleep in the garden yesterday?

2 Could Sally swim with the dolphins?

3 Was there a shark at the zoo?

4 Do monkeys climb better than bears?

5 Can bears swim?

6 Were the elephants the biggest animals at the zoo?

7 Did Zoe's dad walk along the beach yesterday?

8 Could the children feed the parrots at the zoo?

a Yes, they do.

b Yes, they can.

c No, it didn't.

d Yes, they could.

e No, there wasn't.

f Yes, they were.

g No, she couldn't.

h Yes, he did.

 ## Ask and answer.

What's the past of 'drive'?

Drove.

 ## Read and write 'T' (true) or 'F' (false).

1 Lock got a call from a man at the City Zoo. `T`

2 Nick Motors took the lorry from outside the monkey house.

3 Nick Motors rode into the zoo on Lock and Key's motorbike.

4 Lock and Key drove the lorry out of the zoo.

5 Nick Motors knew there was a tiger inside the lorry.

 # Can do

I can say more verbs in the past.

I can talk about animals at the zoo.

I can talk about the biggest, the best and the tallest things.

8 Let's party!

1 Circle the odd one out.

1	**a cup of:**	tea	(bananas)	coffee	milk
2	**a bag of:**	fruit	sweets	potatoes	water
3	**a bowl of:**	soup	salad	noodles	orange juice
4	**a glass of:**	apples	milk	milkshake	lemonade
5	**a bottle of:**	water	pears	sauce	lemonade
6	**a box of:**	cakes	chocolates	chicken	eggs

2 Look and match.

1	There's a	bottle of	coffee.
2	There's a	box of	fruit.
3	There's a	cup of	eggs.
4	There's a	glass of	oranges.
5	There's a	bowl of	water.
6	There's a	bag of	pears.
7	There's a	box of	milk.

Language: expressions of quantity 　　📱 Do the online activities on Practice Extra as you complete this unit.

Look and read. Write sentences.

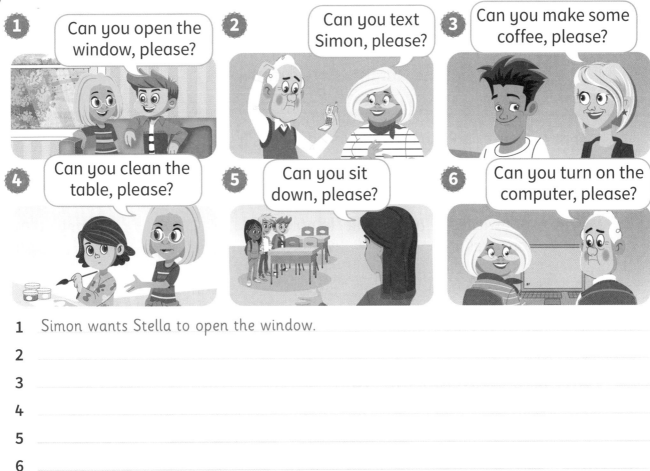

1   Simon wants Stella to open the window.

2 _____

3 _____

4 _____

5 _____

6 _____

2 🎧 10   **Listen, colour and write. There is one example.**

Language: *want someone to (do something)*   **73**

Read, choose and circle.

Last week was
| Jack's |
| Ann's |
| Paul and Mary's |

| ninth |
| tenth |
| eleventh |
birthday.

I went to
| his |
| her |
| their |
party last
| Saturday |
| Wednesday |
| Friday |
. It was
| good |
| exciting |
| nice |
.

We ate
| sushi |
| sandwiches |
| pancakes |
and drank
| fruit juice |
| lemonade |
| water |
. We
| played |
| saw |
| sang |
a funny
| song |
| film |
| game |
.

I gave
| him |
| her |
| them |
| a book |
| a toy |
| a football |
. I came home at
| seven |
| eight |
| nine |
o'clock.

 Look and write 'yes' or 'no'.

1 The man with the moustache is talking the most quietly.   *yes*

2 The younger girl is riding the most carefully.

3 The woman wearing glasses is shouting the most loudly.

4 The boys are riding the best.

5 The older girl is riding the most quickly.

6 The man with the beard is riding the most slowly.

Read and complete the table.

Vicky went to a party yesterday. All the children wore fancy dress. After the party, Vicky's mum wanted to know what each child wore. Can you help Vicky remember?

1 The girl who didn't wear trousers wore a blue hat.
2 The girl who had a black beard wore red trousers.
3 A boy had a big red nose.
4 A girl wore a big black hat.
5 The boy who wore yellow trousers also wore an orange hat.
6 Vicky wore a blue dress.

	trousers	dress	hat	nose	beard
Susan					
Peter					
Vicky			blue		

Who was the clown? ....

Who was the pirate? ....

Who was the nurse? ....

Draw a line through the three words from the same group.
↓ → ↘ ↗

1

panda	lion	giraffe
doctor	worst	bought
film star	drove	nurse

2

model	jumped	longest
kicked	tallest	pirate
best	whale	shark

3

dentist	ate	panda
better	drank	fish
monkey	went	clown

4

pirate	had	snake
could	clown	was
bat	parrot	pop star

1 Read and correct the sentences.

1 She ~~borght~~ bought a big cheese sandwich.

2 I hurt my fut in the pool.

3 We druw a picture for her birthday.

4 We went to the curcus yesterday.

5 Last week, it raind so we didn't play outside.

6 I finished my homewerk so I can dance now.

2 Read and match to make sentences with the same sounds.

1 There was a baboon   a   fly very high.

2 Our kites   b   to do sport.

3 The girl turns   c   with a blue balloon.

4 He walked to the park   d   her purple surfboard.

3 Choose a box. Use the words to write a rhyme.

play	girl	flew	night
day	curly	blue	bike
away	third	new	ride
say	burger	zoo	five
		drew	drive

Movers Listening

1 🎧 11 😊 **Listen and draw lines. There is one example.**

Peter   May   Jack   Kim

Bill   Jane   Paul

How can we write poetry?

Practise

 1 Read and underline the first set of rhyming words in blue and the second set in red.

Listen to my summer <u>song</u>,
Holidays with lots of sun.
Lovely weather all day long,
Making plans to have some fun.

Plan

 Go back to Pupil's Book page 79.

2 Read again and write the words. Read and complete for a new acrostic poem.

S ummer	
U	
N	
N	
Y	

Step 1
Think of a topic for your poem.

Step 2
Choose a 4–5 letter topic word.

Step 4
Think of a word for each letter of your topic word.

Step 3
Write your topic word in the squares.

☐
☐
☐
☐
☐
☐

Write

 3 📝 Use your words to write an acrostic poem.

Edit

 4 Did you …

☐ start each line with the letters of the topic word?
☐ write your poem about the same topic as the word?

Writing Tip

Including a secret word in your poem makes it fun to read and helps readers to understand our ideas.

Literature: How can we write poetry? | 🛡 creative thinking

Do you remember?

1 🎧 12 **Listen and tick the box.**

2 Read and match.

Lock & Key!

1 Nick Motors gave the tiger   a   to see Lock and Key.
2 Lock and Key saw   b   Nick Motors to prison.
3 Nick Motors was happy   c   Lock and Key for catching Nick Motors.
4 The policeman thanked   d   a bag of parrot food.
5 The police took   e   the lorry in the street.

Can do

I can say more food and container words.

I can talk about things I want someone to do.

I can talk about parties.

Review Units 7 and 8

1 **Find and circle the past tense of the verbs.**

~~are~~	find	ride
buy	fly	run
catch	get	say
choose	give	see
come	go	sing
do	have	sit
draw	is	sleep
drink	know	swim
drive	put	take
eat	read	think

w	d	o	f	a	s	r	a	t	o	o	k
a	i	d	l	g	a	v	e	h	i	n	o
s	d	r	e	w	i	d	t	o	m	s	o
b	f	a	w	e	d	r	p	u	a	a	c
g	e	n	i	n	b	o	u	g	h	t	f
c	a	k	e	t	o	v	t	h	a	m	o
a	t	e	r	s	l	e	p	t	d	o	u
u	k	n	e	w	a	t	s	r	a	n	n
g	o	t	s	a	l	c	h	o	s	e	d
h	n	c	a	m	e	a	t	d	a	t	i
t	o	o	w	r	e	a	d	t	n	n	t
w	e	r	e	h	r	o	d	e	g	a	c

2 **Read and tick the picture.**

Frank can't find his bag. Can you help him? His bag has got two books and a box of pencils in it. He's got two small bottles of water, an orange and his favourite comic. Which one is his?

3 **Now describe what's in one of the other bags to your friend.**

4 Circle the odd one out.

1 tired	thirsty	awake	(badly)
2 carry	climbed	copy	cry
3 twelve	third	eighth	twentieth
4 quickly	well	hungry	slowly
5 tea	coffee	juice	vegetable
6 lift	bottle	cup	glass
7 worse	better	quicker	sweater
8 when	which	were	why
9 soup	ate	kebab	sandwich
10 swam	flew	sat	through
11 dolphin	beard	bat	parrot
12 opposite	into	round	sang

5 Use the words from Activity 4 to complete the crossword. Write the message.

1 🎧 13 Listen and number.

1

2 Read and circle.

1 When people help you, …
   a you look at your watch and say, 'Is that the time?'
   b you smile and say, 'Thank you.'
   c you say, 'Can I have an apple, please?'

2 After your birthday party, …
   a you say, 'Thank you' to your parents and help to clean the living room.
   b you sit on the sofa and watch television.
   c you have another piece of cake and play with your new toys.

3 In a café, the man gives you your lunch and says, 'Enjoy your food.' You …
   a look at your lunch and start to eat.
   b smile and say, 'Thank you.'
   c look at your parents and say, 'I don't like cafés.'

4 You're going home after your friend's birthday party. You say, …
   a 'Where's my coat? My mum's here.'
   b 'Can I have that balloon to take home?'
   c 'Thanks a lot. That was a great party.'

Units 3&4 Values Be kind

 Look and write.

> Shall I carry your shopping?   Can you help me, please?
> Would you like some help with your phone?   What's the matter?

 Read and circle.

1 When Jack sees an old person standing on the bus, he always
   sits down / **stands up** for them.

2 When Sally sees a younger child with a problem, she always
   helps / **takes a photo**.

3 When Jim goes to the supermarket with his grandpa, he always **opens** / **carries**
   the shopping bags.

4 When Vicky plays in the park, she always **shares** / **breaks** things with the other
   children.

5 When someone helps Daisy, she always says **'Thank you.'** / **'Goodbye.'**

Units 5&6 Values Be safe

 Look and write. What dangerous things can you see?

1 The woman is listening to music and running into the road.

2 _____

3 _____

4 _____

5 _____

2 **Write the sentences in order.**

1 (It's dangerous) (the road.) (to roller skate on)

It's dangerous to roller skate on the road.

2 (cross the) (You mustn't) (cars.) (road between)

_____

3 (the road at) (must cross) (You) (a zebra crossing.)

_____

4 (near busy) (You mustn't) (roads.) (play)

_____

5 (your bike.) (Wear bright) (helmet on) (colours and a)

_____

Values: units 5 & 6 *Be safe* | social responsibilities

Units 7&8 Values Recycle

1 **Read and match.**

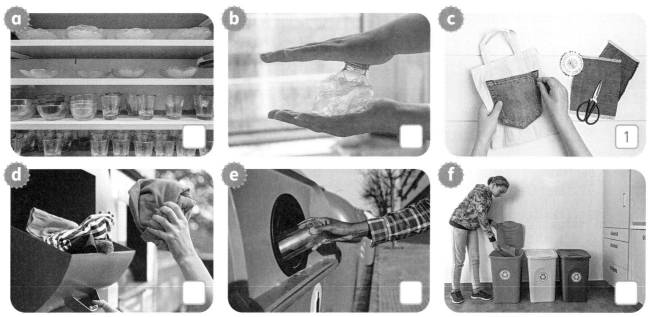

1 We can make new things from old things.
2 Always put glass jars and bottles in a recycling bin.
3 People make bottles, bowls and glasses from recycled glass.
4 Put your rubbish in the correct recycling bins.
5 Make plastic bottles smaller before you recycle them.
6 When you can't reuse old clothes, you can recycle them.

2 **Look and write. What good things are the people doing?**

1 The girl is reusing the clothes.

3 _____

2 _____

4 _____

Grammar reference

Read and complete.

1 I think badminton is _____ than tennis. (easy)
2 My aunt is _____ than my dad. (young)
3 The black cat is _____ than the white one. (thin)
4 Simon's hair is _____ than Stella's hair. (short)

Read and complete. (singing   are   who   's)

1 He's the boy who _____ reading.
2 They're the girls who _____ playing.
3 This is the man _____ works at the hospital.
4 She's the woman who's _____ .

Write the sentences in order.

(dance.) (can) (You) (learn how) (to)

1 _____

(to) (He) (learn) (to swim.) (wants)

2 _____

(to) (It's) (can) (a place) (learn) (you) (sail.) (where)

3 _____

(want) (They) (don't) (to ice skate.) (to learn how)

4 _____

Read and complete. (did   ate   eat   didn't   Yes)

Mum: Did you _____ the sweets?
Tom: _____ , I did.
Mum: How many _____ you have?
Tom: I _____ four sweets.
Mum: Did Dad drink the juice?
Tom: No, he _____ . I drank the juice too!

4 Read and circle.

1 Grandma **danced** / **dancing** yesterday!
2 I **tried** / **trying** to sing the song.
3 She **drop** / **dropped** her books on the floor.
4 We watched the film and **laughs** / **laughed**.

5 Read and circle.

1 I read more **slow** / **slowly** than my brother.
2 He writes more **carefully** / **careful** than her.
3 We are **good** / **better** than them at football.
4 The teacher speaks more **loud** / **loudly** than the pupils.

6 Read and complete.

Today was my birthday and my parents ¹＿＿＿＿＿＿＿＿ (buy) me a mobile phone. I ²＿＿＿＿＿＿＿＿ (put) it in my bag and ³＿＿＿＿＿＿＿＿ (catch) the bus to school. When I ⁴＿＿＿＿＿＿＿＿ (go) into the classroom, I wanted to show my friends, but it wasn't in my bag! The teacher ⁵＿＿＿＿＿＿＿＿ (say), 'Let's help!' Everyone looked for my present, but we couldn't find it. At lunchtime, my brother ⁶＿＿＿＿＿＿＿＿ (bring) me my mobile phone. I didn't put it in my bag, I put it in his!

7 Read and match the questions and answers.

1 Where did you eat lunch?   a I drew three pictures.
2 Who did they see?   b I ate it at school.
3 What did you draw?   c They saw their uncle.

8 Read and complete.

> **best**   **most quickly**   **worst**   **most carefully**

1 Ben writes the ＿＿＿＿＿＿＿＿ in our class. His writing is very neat.
2 My drawing is the ＿＿＿＿＿＿＿＿. It's terrible!
3 My sister swam the ＿＿＿＿＿＿＿＿. She won the race!
4 She plays badminton the ＿＿＿＿＿＿＿＿. She's the champion!

Irregular verbs

Infinitive	Past tense
be	was / were
be called	was / were called
bring	brought
buy	bought
can	could
catch	caught
choose	chose
come	came
do	did
draw	drew
drink	drank
drive	drove
eat	ate
fall	fell
find	found
fly	flew
get	got
get (un)dressed	got (un)dressed
get (up / on / off)	got (up / on / off)
give	gave
go	went
go shopping	went shopping
have	had
have got	had got
have (got) to	had (got) to
hide	hid
hit	hit
hold	held
hurt	hurt

Infinitive	Past tense
know	knew
learn	learned / learnt
lose	lost
make	made
mean	meant
must	had to
put	put
put on	put on
read	read
ride	rode
run	ran
say	said
see	saw
sing	sang
sit	sat
sleep	slept
spell	spelled / spelt
stand	stood
swim	swam
take	took
take a photo / picture	took a photo / picture
take off	took off
tell	told
think	thought
throw	threw
understand	understood
wake up	woke up
wear	wore
write	wrote